PRACTIC

A TREATISE

ON

THE PROPAGATION AND CULTIVATION

OF THE

AZALEA INDICA.

BY

ROBERT J. HALLIDAY,

FLORIST, BALTIMORE, MD.

ILLUSTRATED.

BALTIMORE, MARYLAND.
1880.

BAKER & GODWIN, PRINTERS,
25 Park Row, N. Y.

PREFACE.

Since the publication of Practical Camellia Culture, and the flattering reception of the work, I have been induced to give my practical experience on the cultivation of the Azalea.

In presenting this treatise on the propagation and culture of this plant, of which I claim to be a successful grower, it has been my endeavor to present the subject in as practical a form as possible. The work is complete in itself, and is confined exclusively to the Azalea. The treatment which is embodied within its pages, so far as my knowledge and practical experience extends, is the result of many years of labor, and I believe to be the best method of culture.

This work is intended for the inexperienced florist, for the amateur, and for those who wish to receive some practical hints which may lead them to be successful growers. It gives in detail directions how to grow this plant from a cutting in its different stages, to a plant thirty years old.

I have not omitted or concealed intentionally any knowledge on this subject. All that has been given is the result of careful observation and experience of over twenty years. I have endeavored to give all the directions in plain terms.

Should this work contain some information that will be

valuable to those for whom it has been prepared, or for those of its friends who think it will do good, and save many disappointments, which is the lot, more or less, of all growers of this plant, then will my object be accomplished.

ROBERT J. HALLIDAY.

BALTIMORE CITY, Md., Oct., 1880.

CONTENTS.

CHAPTER I.

CHAPTER II.

CHAPTER III.

CHAPTER IV.

CHAPTER V.

CHAPTER VI.

CHAPTER VII.

CHAPTER VIII.

CHAPTER IX.

CHAPTER X.

CHAPTER XI.

CHAPTER XII.

CHAPTER XIII.

CHAPTER XIV.

CHAPTER XV.

CHAPTER XVI.

CHAPTER XVII.

CHAPTER XVIII.

CHAPTER XIX.

CHAPTER XX.

CHAPTER XXI.

CHAPTER XXII.

CHAPTER XXIII.

CHAPTER XXIV.

CHAPTER XXV.

CHAPTER XXVI.

CHAPTER XXVII.

1*

CHAPTER XXVIII.

CHAPTER XXIX.

CHAPTER XXX.

CHAPTER XXXI.

ILLUSTRATIONS.

11

INTRODUCTION.

The Azalea belongs to the natural order of Ericeæ, and to the sub-order of Rhodorea, named in allusion to the dry places in which many of the species are found, or to the brittle nature of its wood.

Azalea Indica, the well known greenhouse shrub, appears on record as the first specie introduced into Europe from India and China in 1808.

Since that time many new and distinct varieties have been added, of various colors and markings.

Most of our best kinds, with but few exceptions since their introduction from India and China, have been produced by fertilizing, which work has been performed by eminent florists of both Europe and this country.

BALTIMORE, Oct., 1880.

AZALEA CULTURE.

CHAPTER I.

PROPAGATION OF THE AZALEA.—FIVE DIFFERENT MODES OF
INCREASING THE AZALEA.—ARTIFICIAL HEAT NOT NEC-
ESSARY.—WHAT IS NECESSARY TO KEEP THE CUTTINGS
FROM WILTING.—THE CAUSE OF FAILURE TO ROOT THE
CUTTINGS.—PROPER TEMPERATURE.—TIME TO TAKE AZA-
LEA CUTTINGS.—YOUNG AND OLD WOOD PROPAGATION.
—SUITABLE WOOD FOR CUTTINGS.

AZALEAS are increased by the following methods: 1st,
from cuttings of half hardened wood; 2d, by inarching;
3d, by grafting; 4th, from seed; 5th, from sports. The
cuttings are easily managed, all the varieties rooting in
from four to six weeks.

Grafting the Azalea will be found a quick method of
getting a supply of any new variety in a short time.

Inarching the Azalea is seldom practiced by growers of
late years, although it can be done very successfully during
the months of July and August. Azaleas, although easily
grown from seed, are not profitable.

New Azaleas are also produced from sports of established kinds. This way of obtaining new varieties I con-

17

sider a bad freak in our greenhouse kinds of this plant.
See Chapter XVII on this special subject.

My mode of rooting this plant differs entirely from that
of the Camellia. Instead of a bench, use shallow boxes
filled with good sharp sand to receive the cuttings which
are to be rooted. There is no artificial heat necessary for
them.

Give Azalea cuttings the coolest part of the house. It
is not necessary that they should have bottom heat; they
will root more freely without it. A frame will be required
with a glass covering, inside of the house. This extra covering is only needed for a week or ten days. I place the
boxes which are filled with the cuttings in this frame, not
that they be kept close or air-tight, but merely to keep them
from flagging or wilting for the first week or two.

If you wish to be successful in rooting them, keep all
artificial heat away ; never use either top or bottom heat.

Artificial heat has a tendency to produce numerous
insects, therefore keep it away from these cuttings. Red
spider and thrip are the principal causes of failure in a
great many instances.

More Azaleas die from these pests than from any other
cause known.

At the season of the year when the cuttings are placed
in the sand boxes, the days are growing longer and the sun
is becoming more powerful, which will give all the heat that
is necessary during the day.

At night, should the thermometer fall to forty degrees,
they will not be injured, but will be greatly benefited by the
low temperature.

During the day the house should be kept at a temper-ature not over sixty to sixty-five degrees.

I generally take Azalea cuttings from the first to the middle of April.

The young wood must be your guide, for instance, Azalea plants which were placed in the forcing house during November will flower and grow during the first part of January, therefore this wood will be suitable for cuttings during February. Those which have not had the extra heat will probably flower and begin growing during the month of March.

Plants from which I take the cuttings, begin making their young growth about the first of March. When this young wood is from four to six weeks old it is suitable for cuttings, and is what may be termed half hardened wood.

Cuttings can be grown from the old wood in the fall, but not with the same success as those of the young wood in the spring.

In cutting the wood from the plants in the fall much of the bloom is lost, as the shoots used for cuttings at this time is the blooming wood.

My plan and that which I practice is spring propagation, and from the half hardened wood.

The growth of the young wood on the parent plants, when it is half hardened or suitable for cuttings, will be generally about three and a half inches long. Take about two and a half inches of this wood for the cuttings, and only the top shoots, leaving about one inch of the young growth on the parent plant, which will form new shoots and produce flower buds for the coming season.

In taking cuttings from the stock plants do not follow the incorrect practice of pulling the branch, which is intended for the cuttings, from the socket of the old wood, but use a knife for cutting the branches, allowing one inch of the young growth to remain.   With such treatment as this the plants will be shapely.   A clean cut is more easily healed than a ragged or torn one, both in plants and human beings.

CHAPTER II.

For the cuttings use boxes made of one inch boards that
have not been used for any other purpose. I have often
noticed growers using, for propagating purposes, soap, starch
or candle boxes. All such are not fit, they will cause
disease in the cutting bed.

Much depends upon cleanliness in rooting these cuttings.
More Azalea cuttings die from being infected with insects
than from any other cause.

I use boxes which a man can handle without inconven-
ience, 24 inches long by 18 inches wide and three inches
deep. There should be a hole in each corner of about one
inch in diameter, to allow the water to pass off. As there is
more water used for the Azalea cuttings than for any other of
the hard wood class of plants, a half an inch of drainage is
absolutely necessary for their success. You will find this
explained more fully in following chapters.

Fill the boxes with sand, with the exception of the half
an inch at the bottom which has been left for drainage.
Beat the sand with a brick or something weighty. It is
impossible to have it too solid. Water the sand with a fine

21

rose, then beat the second time, not being afraid of having the sand in the boxes too firm.

Fig. No. 1 represents a cutting about two inches and a half long, taken from the parent plant. They can be used shorter, but I have never been very successful with small cuttings. Most growers use the small cuttings, and their success in rooting them is very limited. To be what I call a successful grower of Azalea cuttings is to root and bring from the sand box ninety-five cuttings out of every hundred. Many may think this impossible, as so many unsuc-

Fig. 1. Representing cutting two and a half inches long.

cessful growers are only able to get five living cuttings out of one hundred. But it is done, and can be shown during the months of April and May. If the directions are followed which are contained in this work, there will hardly be a dead cutting in a box which will hold over three hundred.

A very important matter to be looked after in rooting this cutting, is to see that the sand is fresh from the river or bank. It is not necessary to wash it, as so many recommend, but do not use sand that has grown other cuttings. Sand which has been used for some time for propagating purposes, becomes full of vermin, &c. After it has been in the house six months or even less time, if noticed carefully, there will be often found a kind of fungus over the sand and among the cuttings. Many cuttings die from this cause, few growers knowing the reason. Fresh sand and cleanliness are absolutely necessary for the successful propagation of the Azalea, as well as other cuttings.

Figure 2 represents the cutting made and ready for the

sand box. You will notice that four or five of the lower leaves have been removed from the lower portion of the cutting. This portion is inserted in the sand up to where the line is drawn.

The leaves which are left are cut off, as shown in the engraving. Taking half the leaf off is a great advantage to the cuttings, and should not be neglected. The cuttings are generally soft and young, and are very apt to wilt or flag. If wilted so young it is with great difficulty that they recover.

Fig. 2.
Cutting ready for sand box.

In taking cuttings from the stock plants let the wood be of the strongest and most robust kind. All sickly and weak shoots reject. See that they are free from all insects. Do not allow the cuttings to flag or wilt before they are placed in the sand (great care is required here). I usually take the cuttings, in whatever number I wish to grow, place them in a damp cloth with each variety labelled, and after having six or eight varieties so cut, take them to the propagating house and insert them in the sand. The damp cloth will keep the cuttings from flagging until they are placed in the sand.

CHAPTER III.

The cuttings are now ready for the sand boxes which have been prepared. If the sand has been placed in boxes according to the directions already given as regards solidity, it will be necessary to draw straight lines and make openings in the sand to receive the cuttings. To draw straight lines use a carpenter's square or some straight edge. To make the openings in the sand use a knife, place the cuttings in the openings in a straight line one inch deep, then press the sand firmly around each cutting. At the end of each variety place a label with its name, and so on until the box is filled. By following this plan it will not be necessary to use a stick between the varieties, which is often done.

Cuttings thus arranged have a very systematical appearance. It is a very pleasing sight to see the young cuttings in the boxes, in process of rooting, when it is done with neatness and in a practical way. When done in this manner they can be removed when rooted without mixing the different kinds.

When the box is filled with cuttings it should have the

24

appearance of figure 3, which represents a box containing
three hundred cuttings of sixteen different varieties, as will
be noticed by the labels. The box being now filled with

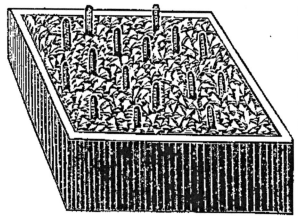

cuttings, a
frame cover-
ed with glass
is required
inside of the
greenhouse.
This frame
is not intend-
ed, as many
would sup-
pose, to keep

Fig. 3.   Box of Cuttings.

them close or partly air-tight, but merely to keep the
young cuttings from flagging or wilting, or, in other words,
to keep the leaves and cuttings erect. If they are allowed
to flag during the first few days, the chances of success are
poor. At no time must the sash be kept close down on
the frame. The first day that the boxes with the cuttings
are put in the frame, keep the sash raised about half an
inch or more. If kept too close they scald and the foliage
turns black. The cuttings will never recover. In propagating always bear in mind that the cuttings at this time
are without roots, and have nothing to support or nourish
the young shoots. The sand which is intended to heal the
the wound causes a callous, and from this the roots will
form, but not without the instructions already given.
Watch the cuttings closely at this time and success will
surely crown your efforts.

2

At night throw up the sash which covers the frame in order to give the cuttings all the air that is circulating through the house.

Figure 4 represents a frame which contains twelve boxes of cuttings. Each box holds three hundred, making in all thirty-six hundred cuttings, which is about the number I grow every season. I grow many Azalea cuttings without the frame, but not with the same success. Therefore I advise using the frame. The second day cover the frame with the sash, as was done on the first day, the sash being raised about one inch. At night throw the sash up. Ventilate in this way until the end of the second week, then remove the sash from the frame entirely. The cuttings should now be erect, and the wood hardened and capable of standing the air which is circulating through the house. Should they flag or wilt during the first week keep them covered more closely. The idea is to keep them erect the first week or two, which can be done by the proper regulation of the frame. Have the glass shaded with whiting. A very important matter to be considered is the syringing, which keeps down red spider, thrip, &c. If these pests get among the Azalea cuttings they will become worthless and only fit for the rubbish heap. Old plants can be cleared of red spider, but I find it impossible to rid this pest from the cutting boxes when it gets fairly started.

To prevent these insects from making their appearance, syringe with clean water morning and night, also wet the sash and boards. Keep a good moisture in the house at all times. Red spider cannot exist in a moist atmosphere.

Syringing will be necessary twice a day until the cuttings are rooted, which will be in six weeks. Water the sand about twice a week, or oftener if required. Watch the sand and do not allow it to become dry.

Important matters to be observed in rooting Azalea cuttings :

Have new boxes filled with clean and fresh sand.

Do not allow the cuttings to flag or wilt for the first week. To avoid this do not keep them too close. This will cause them to scald, damp and turn black. Watch the cuttings several times during the day and you will see what they require.

Keep the strong rays of the sun from them between the hours of ten and four o'clock for the first two weeks, then gradually give more light.

The most important is the syringing. If neglected the cuttings will become covered with red spider, thrip, &c. Many persons fail to root the cuttings on account of neglecting this precaution.

CHAPTER IV.

TIME REQUIRED TO ROOT THE CUTTINGS.—ENGRAVING SHOW-
ING A ROOTED CUTTING. — SOIL IS NECESSARY FOR
CUTTINGS AS SOON AS THEY ARE ROOTED.—HOW TO HAVE
BUSHY OR STANDARD PLANTS.—ENGRAVING OF PLANT
EIGHT WEEKS OLD.—PROPER PLACE FOR CUTTINGS AFTER
BEING ROOTED.

After the cuttings have been in the sand five or six weeks they should be well rooted, having the appearance of figure 5. This cutting has made a half an inch of new wood besides forming roots. It will now need a pot with soil. Do not allow Azalea cuttings to remain in the sand after being well rooted. The roots of this cutting are like thread, and are very numerous, as the engraving shows. They often decay from being kept too long in the sand after being rooted.

Syringing and dampening the foliage, that is necessary to keep the insects down, will cause the roots to rot off of the cuttings if not attended to at the proper time.

After the cutting is well rooted, nothing being in the sand to nourish it, it must have earth. The sand is only intended to heal the wound and root the cutting. The cutting being placed in a two-inch pot, a small portion of the top should be cut off, which will not only cause the young plant

Fig. 5.

Cutting well rooted.

29

to bush and form new shoots but will greatly help to
strengthen the roots.   Potting will retard the growth for a
few days or until the new roots adhere to the fresh soil.
By this treatment the plants will be low and well bushed
from the pot up.

Should standard Azaleas be preferred, or those to resemble grafted plants, then allow the newly-rooted cuttings to
grow without topping until September or the next spring,
when the tops can be taken out and they will bush and form
heads, and have the appearance of grafted plants.

Figure 6 represents a cutting after being removed to a
pot.   It is eight weeks old.   I notice that many growers
(and I have done it myself until experience taught me
better) after taking the cuttings from the sand and placing
them in pots, generally remove them to the benches in the
greenhouse.   This situation will have a fatal effect.   Red
spider and thrip will make sad havoc among them
before September.

My treatment of cuttings after being potted is
to place them in a frame instead of on a greenhouse
bench.   Then cover with sash, which should be
shaded.   Keep them covered with glass from 9
a.m. to 4 p.m., to exclude the strong rays of the
sun, not forgetting that the sash should be removed every day after the sun is off them, that they
may have the full benefit of the night dews.

Fig. 6.   If the dews are not heavy, syringe twice a day

Engraving
of plant night and morning, the same as if they were

eight
weeks old placed in the greenhouse.   A little attention

in a pot. when they are young will fully repay you.   Give

them water at the roots when they require it. Should they want water badly they will wilt, but they should never be allowed to become so dry. Air the frames daily and keep the young plants cool. In dark or rainy weather the sash will not be required over them. Let the cuttings always have the benefit of the showers, as one good shower is worth a dozen artificial waterings. If the proper care has been taken to follow the directions given they will not need any other attention until the middle or last of September.

CHAPTER V.

Fig. 7.
Engraving of plant six
months old.

By the middle or last of September those plants which have been in the frames during the summer will require removing to the benches in the greenhouse. Keep them up within eighteen inches of the glass that they may have all the benefit of the light and air without allowing them to be in a draught. All dead leaves should be removed before bringing them to the house for the winter.

At this time these cuttings which were placed in a two-inch pot during May should have the appearance of

32

figure 7, with two or three shoots on each plant. This growth was made in the frame during the summer. Had they not been topped when potted they would have had only one straight stem.

I always keep Azaleas from cuttings well topped, in order to have them low and bushy. Grafted plants are treated very differently.

The plants now being on the greenhouse bench, syringe twice a day, and water to the roots when dry. The following February or March they will need re potting. They should all be of such a size as to require a three-inch pot. Soon after this they will make their young growth, and by the first of April will be what is termed a one year old plant from a cutting, and should have the appearance of figure 8. Nip the top of the young wood as you did the previous year. These plants should be removed from the greenhouse to the open air in May. Plunge them in sand or any other material that will keep the roots cool during the summer months.

Shade is not necessary after the first year for this plant, as so many recommend. I put them out in the hot scorching sun, being careful that they are removed from the greenhouse on a wet day.

Fig. 8.
Engraving of one year old plant.

The young and old foliage will become hardened by the time the sun strikes them. If put out on a clear day the sun will burn the foliage and the plants will have an unhealthy and unsightly appearance.

Both the Azalea and the Camellia will stand our summer suns if the two precautions are used, putting them out on a wet day and plunging the pot to the rim in the sand.

I do not approve of putting them in the shade under trees, as the drip from them causes many unhealthy plants, which are covered with vermin, &c.

Fig. 9.

One year old plant re-potted and topped.

If the plants have been properly cared for, re-potted and topped, at one year old they should have the appearance of figure 9. Plunge the pots in beds in the open air during May. These plants will make another growth, covering up the unsightly stems which have been topped. Many of them will form buds and bloom the second season. The plants will require no further attention except water-ing, and occasionally, during the months of June, July and August when the night dews are not heavy, syringe once or twice a day. Syringing and dampening the foliage are as important during the summer as if the plants were housed. By September these plants will be eighteen months old, their buds will be formed, but with only one or two flowers on each. Perhaps only one-fourth of your stock will bloom. Flowers should not be looked for on this sized plants; rather encourage them to grow. Although the plants are small and in three-inch pots, they are worth, at present prices for named varieties, ten dollars per hundred. The same retail for twenty-five cents each, or two dollars and forty cents per dozen.

The middle of September the plants should have the appearance of figure 10.

Remove to the greenhouse benches before there is any danger of frost.

Syringe once or twice a day according to the heat in the house.

Young plants of Azaleas thrive best in a cool house.

The following March or April the plants will be two years old and most of them will require a four-inch pot. They each will have perhaps from two to three flowers, as figure 11 represents. They are worth, at wholesale price, fifteen dollars per hundred.

Fig. 10.

Engraving eighteen months old plant.

After making their growth the second season take the the tops from such shoots as are getting long, or from those which give the plant an unsightly appearance.

This wood can be used for cuttings.

Fig. 11.

Engraving two years old plant.

Each plant at this age will produce from six to eight cuttings or five times that number of grafts.

Remove the plants to the open air, plunging them in sand and using the precautions for seting out that were used the previous year, not forgetting to syringe daily.

The fall of this season the plants will be two and a half years old.

They should be well budded and finely shaped, and will command, at trade price, twenty dollars per hundred, or five dollars a dozen, retail.

Figure 12 represents a plant two and a half years old in a four-inch pot, in September. Use the same treatment as for former years.

The third year re-pot all Azaleas that need it during the month of February or March before they make their young growth.

The fresh soil will greatly benefit both the young growth and the flowers.

Top all shoots and use them for cuttings, as you did in previous years. Put the plants outside at the proper time.

Fig. 12.

Engraving two years and a half old plant.

This being the third year, many Azaleas will need five-inch pots; re-pot only those that require it. Let the pots be filled with roots. Keep the plants in good shape by topping. Use the knife freely. Azaleas will grow or break freely from either the young or old wood.

They are not like the Camellia, but will make two growths in one season without injuring the flower buds.

Some Azaleas make a growth in September, and flower the coming season.

Figure 13 represents a plant four years old in a five-inch pot. It is finely budded and well shaped, and will produce about fifty flowers. Give the same treatment as for former years.

Wholesale price of plants this age, four dollars per dozen, or thirty to thirty-five dollars per hundred.

Plants over four years old may only need re-potting once in two years, and as they become older will only need it once in from three to five years. The grower must be the judge of this. If the plants are in a healthy condition and doing well do not disturb them until the roots

Fig. 13.

Engraving of four year old plant.

have extended to the sides of the pot.

When the ground has soured, the drainage has become imperfect, and the plants are not in a healthy condition. Reduce the ball of earth, give fresh drainage and a smaller pot. Do not give large pots to sickly plants.

Encourage them to make new roots. Azaleas shed or lose many of their leaves in the fall and winter, and many persons imagine their plants are dying. This is natural to the plant (half deciduous). They will fill up this nakedness with fresh green foliage the following season.

When Azaleas are in an unhealthy condition their foliage becomes a yellowish-green, and they grow very slowly or not at all. Old plants may be dying for years before they are noticed by those who have had a limited experience.

Fig. 14.
Engraving of a five year old plant.

Figure 14 represents a well grown plant of good shape, five years old from a cutting. It is grown in such a way that it can be trimmed up to one straight stem.

There are other varieties of the low growing kind, which are better-grafted if you wish them to form heads on straight stems.

Fig. 15.

Engraving of a five year old plant, trimmed up.

Figure 15 represents the same plant five years old from
a cutting, with stem trimmed up to give it the appearance
of a grafted plant. Any of the strong growing varieties
can be trimmed in this way.

CHAPTER VI.

I am often asked which I prefer, the grafted plants of the Azalea or those grown from the cuttings. I grow largely of this plant, and practice both growing from cuttings and from grafting. Sometimes I inarch, but very seldom. I have a preference, not that one way is better than the other in respect to flowering, for there is no difference in this particular, but there is a difference in the appearance of the plants after they are five years and older. As this is only a matter of taste, each grower of the Azalea must decide for himself.

I prefer the grafted plants for one reason only : if they receive the proper attention and the young shoots are pinched or topped often, they will form beautiful round heads on stems twelve to fifteen inches from the pot, and when in flower will be an ornament for the conservatory, parlor or greenhouse. Large plants can be grafted with several different kinds on one plant, but I prefer to graft the young plant and with only one variety.

The old plants cannot be grafted with the same success as the young ones, and further, they cannot be as shapely as those which are grafted on the stock one year old.

Many varieties that grow strong from cuttings can be trimmed up and have the appearance of those that are

41

grafted with fine round heads by pinching the young shoots
and keeping them up to one straight stem.

Of all plants I grow, and of all methods of increasing
them, there is none so interesting as grafting the young
Azalea. It is so easily performed, and with such great success, that there is seldom found a dead one in five hundred.

Keep a supply of plants on hand of the white
variety named Indica Alba, to use as a stock on which to
graft, or the variety named Phœnicia, which makes equally
as good a stock to graft upon. I prefer Indica Alba, for the
reason that the plants are always valuable, while those of
Phœnicia are worthless as regards flowers.

By keeping a few of these stocks on hand the grower
will have a quick way of getting a supply of any new kind
which may be introduced.

Most of our new varieties of Azaleas are imported from
Europe.

It is the aim of all importers and growers of this plant
to get the new kind propagated early by means of grafting.
This can be done if the stocks are in condition, and there
is young wood on the newly-imported variety. By the
process of grafting, plants can be in condition to sell in six
weeks after the parent plants have been imported.

These small grafted plants, with probably one inch of
the new kind on the stock growing, will oftentimes command a higher price than those of the older varieties three
and four years old.

It is not the size or age that causes them to sell at a high
figure, but it is some new variety that has never been in
our collection.

It is therefore the interest of all growers to procure the new kinds as early as possible, in order to be able to offer them as soon as they are in demand.

Azalea stocks should always be kept on hand.

My reason for recommending Indica Alba in preference to Phœnicia for a stock is that they can be grown as other varieties, and the plants and flowers are always salable, even should you not wish to graft all the stock of Alba you have on hand.

Phœnicia is equally as good for a stock, but the flowers which are a dark purple have no demand, and are really worthless after they are too old to be used as a stock.

CHAPTER VII.

Grafting the Azalea differs entirely from the Camellia. The stock on which I graft is Indica Alba, the old single white. Although I use this for a stock, I consider it the best single white in my collection for flowers and for early forcing. It should be grown largely by those who grow for profit. It is easily rooted, of quick growth, and makes a strong stock.

Grow this variety precisely the same as the other kinds, with one exception : make the cuttings a little longer, say about three inches. Remove two or three leaves from the bottom of the cutting, as represented in figure 16 ; place in boxes. In previous chapters will be found full directions for rooting this cutting.

Figure 17 represents a cutting of Indica Alba rooted. It is five weeks since it was placed in the sand.

It has made a growth of half an inch, which will be seen by the engraving. If this plant is wanted to be used, on which to graft the new kind, do not remove the top.

Fig. 16.

Cutting three inches long.

If to be grown without grafting, I would advise the top to be pinched out when potted, in order to make a bushy plant.

44

Fig. 17.
Cutting of
Indica Alba
rooted.

If for grafting allow the top to grow, and in four weeks after being potted this plant will be in a suitable condition to graft.

The young wood of the imported kinds, which is suitable to graft on this stock, will at this time be found very scarce, as the young growth has been made and buds are forming for the next season's flowering. Therefore this hardened wood is not suitable to use for grafts.

My practice is to grow the stock until the following February or March, when it will be one year old, and then graft upon it. Keep the stocks in the smallest size pots until after they are grafted.

CHAPTER VIII.

I advise the Azalea to be grafted in February and March.

Where the florist's business is conducted properly, there are certain months for performing the different modes of propagation. The plants from which the wood is taken must be your guide in regard to the proper time. For instance, I am most successful in grafting the Azalea during the months of February or March, when the wood, both graft and stock, is very young.

I usually work about three thousand plants at this time.

I also practice grafting at other times during the year, but in limited quantities, and not with the same success as in the months recommended.

Most Azaleas seen with fine round symmetrical heads on a bare stem of twelve inches from the pot, are grafted plants.

Do your grafting of this plant during February and March. At this time the imported kinds will be showing their young shoots. The stocks will also be in fine condition for this work. The wood being very young, great care must be exercised so as not to allow the young graft to wilt or flag before or after it is worked.

46

For grafting there is a frame or box needed inside the greenhouse, with two coverings of glass.

Place the frame inside of the house, putting a sash or a covering of glass over it. Inside of the frame nail strips on the sides, having them extend across the frame, or in any way that you may think best, so as to allow another covering of glass. I use for this inside covering single panes of glass.

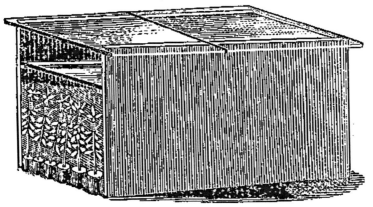

Fig. 18.
Box for grafting.

Figure 18 represents a box frame, showing grafts, and also the coverings needed.

For persons who do not graft in large quantities a bell glass will answer.

When grafted in large quantities a frame is needed, and a double covering of glass is really necessary, as it is impossible to keep a sufficient quantity of air from them with only the sash.

Use the double covering and your success will be sure.

Exclude the air as much as possible from the young grafts.

The younger the wood of both stock and graft, the more easily they will unite.

If properly done, the directions being followed, they will unite in forty-eight hours.

By many, the time may be considered very short for a graft to unite to the stock. As I have remarked before, in the rooting of the cutting, it is done and can be shown.

One very important point in grafting this plant is to have young wood, as it unites more readily.

Keep them close for two weeks, when the panes of glass can be removed from the inside of the frame. Then with good shading and the one covering of glass they should not wilt or flag. Should they show a tendency to flag, put the glass back again that was removed. Keep their heads erect.

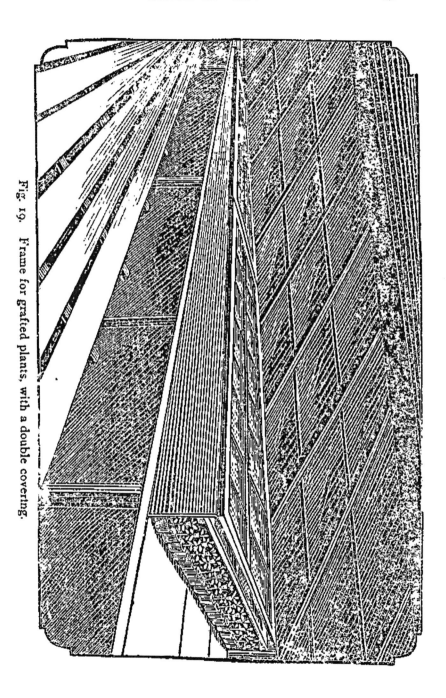

Fig. 19. Frame for grafted plants, with a double covering.

3

Figure 19 represents my frame for grafting inside of the greenhouse.

Make the frame to suit the number of plants that are to be grafted.

The engraving shows frame forty feet long by three feet wide, twelve inches high. It will accommodate three thousand plants, which is the number I generally graft in February and March.

Notice the two coverings. This is all necessary to grow graft for plant.

To grow seventy-five out of one hundred is not what I call a success. Many growers would be satisfied with this number. I want ninety-five out of one hundred, or there has been a lack of attention.

With all the coverings of glass that I have recommended, the frame is not air-tight, nor do we wish it so, but it will tend to keep enough air away from them to unite the graft.

Keep the sash well darkened with whiting. It is not necessary to whiten the single panes of glass that are inside.

CHAPTER IX.

ENGRAVING SHOWING STOCK SUITABLE FOR GRAFTING.—HOW TO GRAFT.—ENGRAVING SHOWING HOW TO INSERT THE GRAFT.—ENGRAVING SHOWING PLANT GRAFTED.—DIRECTIONS FOR GRAFTING.

Figure 20 represents the Azalea stock, which is one year old, in a two-inch pot. Plant six inches high.

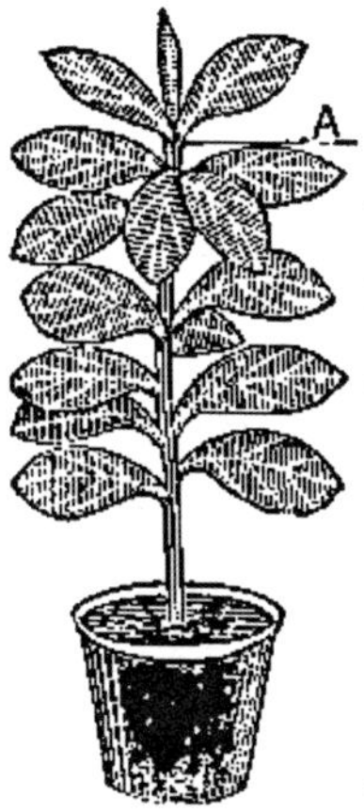

Fig. 20.
Stock one year old.

Notice in the engraving where the line is drawn and marked A. This is where the top should be taken from the plant to insert the graft. The smallest particle is only taken off.

The stocks are not fit to graft upon if they are not in a growing state, and having young wood on the tip ends where the grafts are to be placed. The graft which is to be inserted in this stock must also be of the young wood.

The younger the wood is of both, the surer the success.

Do not cut the top from the stocks before you are ready to place the grafts on them.

The same care should be taken of the grafts, not forgetting that a newly-made wound, if bandaged and attended to immediately, is more quickly healed than one which has remained open some time.

Use none but good healthy plants for stocks. Let the grafts be the same.

Figure 21 represents the stock with the top taken off, the opening is made in the stock and the graft placed. I use what is termed by florists a wedge graft. Cut the stock right through the middle of the stem, as the engraving shows, but only allow this cut to be a quarter of an inch or less down. A good knife is best to use here.

Take the young graft which is intended for the stock, not allowing it to be more than half an inch in length. Slice the smallest portion of wood from each side. If the graft is so young and soft that the knife will not pare it, then scrape it. Only the smallest portion of the wood is to be taken from the piece which is intended for the graft.

Fig. 21.

How to insert the graft.

Insert the graft and tie with thread, and it should have the appearance of figure 22. This operation is now complete.

As soon as there are a dozen, or even less, grafted, remove them to the frame.

The wood being very soft they will not stand erect long without being in a close place.

If they wilt down at this time, both labor and time have been spent for nothing.

Keep them erect for the first three days, and success is certain. After the plants have been grafted ten days or two weeks, remove the single panes or the inside covering of glass, keeping the sash over them three weeks longer, then gradually give them air.

The first day raise the sash a half inch, closing it at

night for one week, after this time allow more air, gradually hardening them off. After the fifth or sixth week the sash can be removed from the frame.

The grafts will now be firmly united, and the unions hardened.

The thread which held the grafts in position should now be taken off. It is not necessary to tie the graft again like hard wood grafting.

Fig. 22.

Graft inserted and tied.

At this time the stock which has been newly grafted will have a tendency to throw out shoots below the graft. All such shoots should be removed at once. The newly-inserted graft is the only portion of the plant that should grow.

It will not be necessary to syringe the grafted plants while they are in the frame. They will receive ample moisture from the glass, caused by keeping the frame close. Oftentimes there is too much moisture in the frames. Obviate this by ventilating twenty or thirty minutes, or just long enough to dry the extra moisture in the frame. This dampness often proves disastrous to the young graft, therefore care and watchfulness must be exercised at this time.

CHAPTER X.

ENGRAVING OF PLANT SIX WEEKS AFTER BEING GRAFTED.—
ENGRAVING OF GRAFTED PLANT WITH THE TOP NIPPED
OUT.—TIME TO RE-POT YOUNG GRAFTED PLANTS.—THREE
ENGRAVINGS OF PLANTS TWO, THREE, AND FOUR YEARS
FROM GRAFT.

Figure 23 represents a plant six weeks after being
grafted. The graft is firmly united to the stock. It has
made a growth of about two inches before the thread
has been taken off. These plants will all
require re-potting. Give them three-
inch pots, which is one size larger than
those in which they have been grafted.
Fresh soil at this time will encourage the
grafts to grow.

Fig. 23.
Graft firmly
united.

Remove these to the open air in May.
Plunge the pots in sand, taking the necessary precaution to set them out on a wet
day.

Nip the tops from the grafts before
putting them outside, and they will have
the appearance of figure 24. These
plants require nothing further for the summer except water
at the roots when dry, and syringe once or twice a day.

Occasionally during the summer nip the tops, in order
that they may begin early to form heads.

Remove to the greenhouse in September. Syringe once

54

a day until the next spring, February or March, when the plants will be one year old from grafts, or two years old from cuttings. At this time they will require re-potting, and should be ready for four-inch pots. Many of them should produce from two to four flowers.

A portion of the young growth that they will make this spring can be used for cuttings or grafts. This will also tend to give them fine heads for the following fall, with flower buds. Remove to the open air in May, as before.

The coming fall, which is the second year from graft or the third year from cutting, they should be finely shaped and well budded, and should have the appearance of figure 25. At present prices they are worth twenty-five dollars per hundred, trade price.

Fig. 24.
Grafted plant topped.

The same retail at fifty cents a piece, or five dollars a dozen.

Treat as described for the previous winter.

The spring of the following year the plants should be good, producing from twenty to forty flowers.

The plants at this age will give quantities of cuttings and grafts.

Many of them will require five-inch pots.

Keep the plants well topped with a view of having good round heads for the fall of the third year. They should have somewhat the appearance of figure 26. The fall of this the third season from the graft, the plants will be shapely, and of good size, well covered with flower

Fig. 25.

Plant two years from graft.

buds, and will be becoming valuable. Trade price, from forty to fifty dollars per hundred; retail price, one dollar each.

The following spring, which is the fourth year from grafts, they should flower profusely, in fact, in such quantities that but little of the foliage will be seen when they are in bloom.

Grafted plants are worth more, and are sold at a higher figure at this age, than those of the same age grown from cuttings.

Grafted plants form beautiful heads.

The cost of handling makes the difference in price between the two methods of propagating.

Figure 27 represents a well-grown plant, with a fine head, and covered with flower buds. It is four years old from graft, and should measure in diameter from fourteen

Fig. 26.

Plant three years from graft.

to sixteen inches. This is a handsome plant for the green-house, conservatory, or for exhibition. The trade price, seventy-five dollars per hundred; retail price, one dollar and fifty cents each.

Fig. 27. Plant four years from graft.

3*

CHAPTER XI.

Plants of this age are easily managed, and require but little attention, compared to many other plants. All Azaleas of this size, in re-potting, should be well drained. Broken pots, oyster shells, or any hard material, will answer, that will allow the water to pass out without clogging up the holes which are in the bottom of the tubs or pots.

I consider drainage an important matter for all plants that are not re-potted every season. (See chapter on drainage.)

All Azaleas, both large and small, should be put out in the open air during the summer months. As remarked before, it is not necessary to give them shade, but care should be taken to place the plants outside on a wet day.

Azaleas are somewhat like Camellias, they have a time for making their young growth, after which they form buds, and flower the coming fall and winter.

One advantage Azaleas have over the Camellias: they will make a young growth in the spring. While in flower, part of this young wood can be taken for cuttings or grafts. The plants will break again and make a second growth from the old and young wood. This will not in any way inter-fere with the flowering of the plant the coming season.

Water plants of this size and age when dry at the roots, giving them enough to wet every root and fiber.

When the soil is dry it will have a white appearance.

Syringe often, never less than once a day.

They are subject to red spider, thrip, &c.

I have yet to see a collection of Azaleas that are entirely free from these pests during the months of March and April, just before they are put in the open air. If syring-ing is attended to properly, they will not be found in such large quantities as to cause the plant to be unhealthy. They will all disappear soon after being brought out in the open air. Heat and moisture are sure death to these insects. (See chapter on insects.)

During the months of March and April, while the Aza-leas are under glass, it will be necessary to have the glass partly shaded, to keep the strong rays of the sun from burning the young foliage. Do not put a dark cover over them, as is often done.

All plants require light, the same as human beings, but not the strong rays of the sun between the hours of 10 a.m. and 3 p.m.

To exclude the rays of the sun use a wash for the glass of linseed oil and turpentine; this will be sufficient shade.

Figure 28 represents a well grown and finely shaped plant of Indica Alba, grown from a cutting.

· This plant measures five feet in height, and four feet in diameter. It will produce one thousand or more flowers

Fig. 28.

Indica Alba, from a cutting.   A well grown plant. four feet in
diameter.

annually. Plants of this size are rarely sold. It pays the owner to keep them for the flowers.

The plant, which will be seen in engraving 28, is in a fine healthy condition.

This variety, old Indica Alba, the single white flower, is to Azaleas what the Alba Plena is to Camellias, being the best for profit. Taking all its qualities into consideration, it roots freely, is a robust grower, a sure and profuse flowerer. It is one that is easily forced for early flowers, and not affected or injured by the extreme heat of the forcing house, and lastly, I consider it the best one to grow to use as a stock upon which to graft. The plant, when young, is always strong and erect. This quality in a stock is not found in all varieties of Azaleas.

There are many other good single white Azaleas, better than the Alba in some respects, but they do not possess the combined qualities of the Indica Alba.

The cut flowers of the Azalea, which are open, are worth but little to send any distance.

The buds can be sent in safety when the time does not exceed three days. For home consumption the open flowers are valuable and indispensable.

CHAPTER XII.

Forcing is what may be termed giving the plants extra artificial heat to cause them to bloom early.

I know of no plant which can stand more heat than the Azalea, without becoming sickly. If you wish them to flower early, they can be kept at a temperature of ninety to one hundred degrees without any bad effect to the plant, providing they are syringed often, never less than twice a day, watering at the roots when they require it.

Or this plant will thrive in a cool-house where the thermometer does not get below forty degrees.

Kept at this low temperature they will not bloom before March or April.

This interesting group of plants adorns the greenhouse, hot-house, conservatory, or parlor, during the dull months. They should be cultivated in such a way as to be made to bloom from November to May, by having a succession of plants.

Those that you wish to bloom early should be brought to the forcing house the first of September.

The first season it will perhaps be difficult to bring the plants into flower before the middle or last of December. After this year there will not be any trouble in forcing them to bloom the first part of November. The plants which bloomed the past season in December will make their growth and form their buds for the next season's flowering, before those which have been kept in the cool-house will have made their flowers.

When forcing this plant do not allow it to be checked by giving an extra quantity of air. Both light and air are beneficial to all plants, and the Azalea needs much of it, but they will not stand a draught at this time. Care is also required after they have flowered.

Those that have been in the forcing house when making their young wood should not have a check, as it will greatly interfere, not only with the health of the plant, but the bloom for the coming season will be limited, some plants, perhaps, having no bloom.

The flowers which these forced plants will produce will not be as large in size as those which have been kept cool, neither will the colored varieties be as bright in color, but the advantage of having them bloom early will be of greater value.

This plant is well adapted for both the hot or cool greenhouse, and is capable of enduring a very high temperature without injury, providing syringing and watering is properly attended to. Do not forget that red spider thrives in a hot and dry atmosphere; it cannot exist long where heat and moisture are combined.

In forcing Azaleas a good exposure to light is necessary.

Never crowd them.

Admit air in mild weather.

Do not allow them to have a check while being kept at a high temperature.

CHAPTER XIII.

In former chapters will be found all the necessary directions for taking the cuttings, the time to place them in the sand, and the proper attention to be given them.

For amateurs not growing this cutting in large quantities, I will show a box most suitable for their cuttings, in engraving 29. This box is ten inches wide, fifteen inches long, and three inches deep, holding seven varieties of Azaleas, as will be noticed by the labels in the engraving.

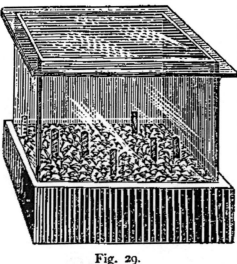

Fig. 29.

Box for Cuttings.

Make the box to suit the number of cuttings that are to be grown.

This box, represented in figure 29, has the appearance of a tight glass case, but it is nothing but four panes of common glass pressed to the bottom of the box; the sand holds the four panes in position without any other support. The covering is a

64

single pane laid on the top of the four. A box arranged in this way will answer as well as a frame for rooting the cuttings. The box, when covered, is by no means air-tight, but many would imagine it so.

If they were kept perfectly air-tight they would damp, the young foliage becoming black, and the cuttings would be worthless. The covering is merely intended to keep a portion of air from the young cuttings, and prevent them flagging or wilting for the first week. After this time all the glass must be removed.

The first day the cuttings enter the sand keep them close. After this keep the top pane elevated to admit some air. Watch the young cuttings, and if they flag badly there is too much air circulating about them.

Let the sand that is used be clean and fresh from bank or river. The boxes or pans must be new.

Cleanliness is a very important matter to be considered in the cutting bed.

Keep the boxes in a cool place. Syringe with clean water twice a day.

In former chapters will be found other instructions if they are needed.

CHAPTER XIV.

There are few plants that add more beauty to the amateur's conservatory than grafted Azaleas, with heads of perhaps fifteen inches in diameter, on a bare stem twelve to fifteen inches from the pot, or those that are grown from cuttings which will be low and bushy from the pot up, covered so profusely with flowers that the foliage is scarcely seen.

I cannot understand why it is, that among so many amateur growers, and those who have private greenhouses, there are so few who have shown a preference for some of the *improved* varieties of this plant.

The old Phœnicia, a miserable common purple, and many others just as worthless, will be found in almost every greenhouse.

Azaleas are not difficult to propagate or grow, neither is the price high, considering the time and care bestowed upon them by the grower.

Blooming plants can be bought at any establishment, for from fifty cents and upwards, according to the size.

A plant from three to five years old, with fine heads, and such that will produce one hundred or more flowers, will cost from one dollar and fifty cents to three dollars each, or fifteen to twenty dollars a dozen. Plants this size will be very ornamental to the conservatory.

66

In many collections, where this plant is not grown for profit, will be found not only miserable varieties, but often long, straggling looking plants of some of the more improved kinds, that have become so through neglect to prune. These can be gotten in shape by using the knife freely, just after they have flowered. They will form new shoots from both the old and young wood.

Trim the worthless kind, in any collection, up to one straight stem, and, during the months of July and August, inarch some of the more improved kinds on them, and in two or three years you will have a fine variety with good heads.

Former chapters will show how amateurs should graft, also how to grow the cuttings for stocks.

When there is a limited quantity to be grafted, use a bell glass in place of a frame, as figure 30 represents. This glass will accommodate twelve grafted plants; the stocks are one year old in two-inch pots.

Use only the tip ends of the shoots for grafts, and also the tip ends of the stock where the graft is to be inserted.

The engraving in the chapter on grafting will show how to cut and bandage.

It will be only a few days before they unite, and in three or four weeks the bell glass can be removed. About the third week give some air to harden the young grafts, so that they will not wilt when the covering is taken off.

Fig. 30.
Bell glass with grafted plants.

Grafting will be found very

interesting for amateur cultivators of this plant, the work is so easily performed, and with good success.

Three or four days' time will decide whether they are going to unite. Do not forget that the younger both the graft and the stock is, the more successful you will be. After the plants are grafted the stocks will throw out shoots below the graft; rub these off, and allow nothing to grow but the newly-inserted graft. One year old healthy stocks are the most suitable to use for grafting. Do not attempt to graft old plants. It can be done, but it will be better to allow experienced growers to do it. Amateurs had better work old plants by inarching.

CHAPTER XV.

Growers of late years seldom practice inarching, unless they have some inferior varieties which are too large to use as stock on which to graft. They then resort to this means of working an improved kind upon them.

I presume all persons who have this work, also have Practical Camellia Culture, which will give all necessary engravings, &c., showing how to cut, bandage, &c.

Inarching the Azalea is done in every way like that of the Camellia but it will unite and knit together in four weeks ; the Camellia will take two weeks longer.

The only objection I have to inarching this plant is that it has to be done inside the greenhouse, during the hot months of July and August, to make it a success. Great care must be given them.

The foliage must be dampened often to keep red spider from infecting them, as it would be some time before you could rid the newly inarched plants of this pest.

It is more profitable to grow the young stocks and graft, than to waste time and labor in inarching the old plants of Azaleas.

The amateur cultivator may be more successful in inarching than he would be in grafting.

I have not practiced inarching for many years. Growing from cuttings and grafting have been my methods for increasing this plant, and I advise all others to adopt the same.   69

CHAPTER XVI.

I have given the different methods for increasing the Azalea by cuttings, grafting, and inarching. I will now give the process of producing the seedlings.

Most of the new varieties of all plants are produced from seed, but there are many new varieties of the Azalea which have originated from sports (of which I will give an account in the following chapter).

If you wish to grow from seed, which is easily done, first save the seed from the best varieties only, and from the flowers that have been fertilized with the pollen of some other good kind. Let the seed be only from good, strong, robust varieties, and those which produce good flowers, that the young progeny may have a good constitution.

In growing seedlings, every one has some expectation of getting something new and distinct from all others.

Those plants from which seeds are to be produced should not be syringed after they are in flower, or when fertilized or impregnated with other kinds.

As soon as the flowers fade, the seed vessel will be formed in the calyx of the dead flower. It will resemble a small pea. Quite a number of seeds will be found in this, although it may be four months, and sometimes longer, before the seeds are ripe and fit to plant.

Gather when ripe, and sow at once in shallow pans, or

70

boxes. The seed being very minute, judgment must be used not to sow too deep, also be careful that the seed is not floated away by heavy watering.

Keep the pans or boxes in a house with moist heat. Never allow the soil to become dry. Cover them with panes of glass, which remove when you see the seedlings making their appearance, or they will damp and mould away.

When the seedlings are large enough to handle, pick them out of the pans, give them new pans and fresh soil. After this they can be removed to pots, and treated the same as cuttings of the same age.

The third year most of the seedlings will bloom. Among them may be found some new and valuable varieties.

I do not practice growing this plant from seed, nor do I advise others to do so. I prefer giving this privilege to European growers, purchasing the good kinds from them after they are named, and the worthless kinds have been picked out.

The worthless kinds generally predominate in a lot of seedlings.

In raising seedlings, many suppose they will get all good kinds, but such is not the case. You are apt to get a great many inferior sorts. You are fortunate if you get one good distinct kind from one hundred seedlings. If the precautions are taken to fertilize one good kind with another, many good varieties worth growing may be secured, but a few only can be named, as they will be found to be similar to many varieties already established and named.

CHAPTER XVII.

AZALEA SPORTS.—WHY THEY SHOULD NOT BE ENCOURAGED.

Those who are familiar with growing the Azalea are aware that many of our new and best varieties have not been produced by the ordinary way of procuring them, which is from seed. Many of the new, best, and most distinct kinds have appeared as sports.

A named or established variety often produces here and there a type on one branch entirely different from the original flowers, and when this branch is taken from an established kind of Azalea and propagated, it generally holds good.

This is unlike many sports of plants of a different character.

By this means many, and I may say most of the new varieties have been produced, instead of from seed, as in the way of producing new varieties of most other plants.

Amateurs, or those who cultivate this plant for its beauty while in flower, will, I have no doubt, be very much pleased when they find two or three different kinds of flowers on the same plant, which are entirely distinct from the established kind and the one which they purchased. The majority of the flowers, though, will be the same as the established variety.

These sports seldom appear on small plants.

The sporting of Azaleas cause the growers much annoyance, and is considered a bad feature in the plant.

72

We will take, for instance, the established variety named Admiration. If the old stock plant is not watched when in flower, and the sporting branches cut away, from this one kind will be propagated four other distinct sorts.

I have noticed the following kinds on Admiration : Glory of Belgium, Criterion, Marginata, and Iveryana, or others similar to those named. By this way it is with difficulty that the grower can keep his stock genuine. Great care must be exercised to remove the sports, being careful to watch the plant when in bloom.

The variety named Barckleyana has produced from sports over twenty kinds. Had all these sports been of a better variety than the established one, it would not cause so much annoyance. The sports are often very inferior. Therefore 1 am one, with many other growers, that do not like to see this freak in this greatly admired plant.

Watch the plant closely when in flower, especially those kinds from which the stock is grown.

As soon as they are seen giving to a sport, immediately take the whole branch or twig out. This is the only means of keeping the stock true to the established kind.

All growers are careful to have the stock plants true to name, and without the precautions are taken which have been given, the stock of Azaleas cannot be relied upon.

I will here give another instance of its sporting qualities. Azalea Variegata is a variegated flower, or pink margined, or blotched white, or of several colors, and also one of the first of our Chinese varieties.

4

Lateritia, which is a regular brick dust color, will often be found on it.

We propagate this and send it out under the name of Variegata.

The purchaser may think, if he does not say, that we send out spurious kinds, or those not true to name. When they order Azalea Variegata they do not want it to turn out Azalea Lateritia, a brick dust color.

The grower in this way often gets a bad name when he is not deserving of it.

This chapter will show why I do not like sports on the Azalea, and at the same time explains to the purchaser why he sometimes gets a different color from the one he ordered.

CHAPTER XVIII.

AZALEAS FOR THE AMATEURS OR THOSE WHO HAVE A SMALL
COLLECTION.—TREATMENT FOR THE SAME.

There are few plants grown that are more worthy of a place in the amateur's collection than the Azalea, for ornamenting and beautifying the greenhouse. Its brilliancy of color and markings, with many delicate shades of flowers, and also blooming, as it does with ordinary treatment, from December to June, renders it a universal favorite.

There are but few hard-wooded plants which the amateur can grow and bloom with as much satisfaction as the Azalea.

They are capable of enduring a high and intense heat without injury, if they are syringed twice a day, or this plant can be grown in a house where the thermometer does not fall below forty. In this temperature they can be made to bloom abundantly.

Do not crowd the plants.

Give plenty of light and air on all sides.

Those which are grown with a variety of plants, and at a high temperature, will need their foliage dampened often. They will bloom during January and February.

Those which have been kept cool will bloom during March and April. Manage the plants so as to have a succession of flowers from November until May. (See previous chapters for fuller directions.)

Look over the stock when through flowering, re-pot all

those whose roots have extended to the sides of the pots, and those which are in an unhealthy condition, or with soil sour, reduce the ball of earth. Give fresh drainage, and place back in a smaller pot or tub. Encourage them to make new roots. Prune the tops well back.

Use the knife freely. Cut old or young wood away, and get the plants shapely.

Old plants will not need re-potting more than once in two or three years. See that the drainage is good, so the water may pass off from the roots.

Examine every plant when through flowering. It is not necessary to take them all out of the pots or tubs. The tops of the plants will usually tell what they need.

When re-potting much twiggy and weak wood will be found in the center of the plants. All such cut away; it is only robbing the good shoots of the nourishment they require.

Syringe the plants twice a day during the months of March and April. Remove them from the greenhouse to the open air as early in May as is practicable.

Do not place them under trees, as the drip therefrom is very injurious, and will cause them to be covered with red spider in the fall. Remove them from the house on a rainy day, so there will be no danger of the sun burning the foliage.

Plunge the pots in sand to keep the roots cool.

Do not plunge the pots into the earth, and more especially hard-wooded plants, or those which are only re-potted once in a long time, as the earth soil becomes full of worms, causing the soil to sour and the plants to lose their roots.

Worms will not work in sand.

It is not necessary to give the plants shade; they can be placed in the sun without injury.

Follow the directions for syringing the foliage of the plants which are outside in summer, and they will be greatly benefited.

All plants that do not need re-potting, take one inch of soil from the top of the ball, replenishing it with fresh soil. This is what is termed by florists top dressing the plant without removing it from the pot or tub.

Remove the plants to the greenhouse about the middle of September, before there is any danger of frost. See that they are free from all insects, and all dead leaves pinched off. After they are placed in the house, give every plant a good watering with lime water, which will kill all worms and keep the ground sweet.

Keep the glass shaded during the months of March and April, to prevent the foliage from burning. Use a wash for shading the glass composed of the following :—One gallon of turpentine, one pint of boiled linseed oil, well mixed. It can be applied to the glass with an ordinary paint or whitewash brush.

CHAPTER XIX.

AZALEAS FOR WINDOW CULTURE.—THE PROPER TEMPERATURE REQUIRED.—ENGRAVING OF AN ELASTIC SPRINKLER.—ENGRAVING OF COAL OIL STOVE FOR SMALL CONSERVATORY.

I have frequent inquiries from correspondents; will the Azalea do for windows or house culture?

I know of no plant more beautiful for window decoration than the Azalea is when in full bloom.

The success with this plant is much better than that of the Camellia. It will stand a great amount of heat, but at the same time a moist atmosphere is necessary for it.

Dampening the foliage three times a day will give all the moisture that is necessary.

There will be very little trouble in growing or flowering this plant in a window that is inclosed.

I would advise those who grow these plants in windows, to keep them at a temperature of from fifty to fifty-five degrees, and the plants will come into bloom during February.

Those grown with extra heat will require double the amount of care and attention than those that are grown in a low temperature.

All plants do best, and are healthier, that get but little artificial heat.

In fine weather air the plants freely.

If intended to grow in the windows, do not remove them to the house until late in the fall, or just before frost. Place them outside early in the spring. About once a month take the plants from the window and dip their heads into a solution of the following wash :—8 gallons of soap suds, ¼ lb. of sulphur, and a little soft soap, well mixed together. After being dipped into this solution, a soapy gloss will cling to the foliage, which will not be objectionable. Syringing with clean water will remove most of the insects that infest this plant.

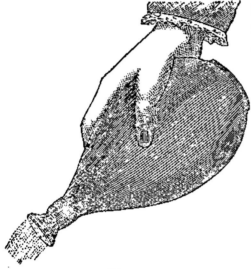

Fig. 31.

Elastic Sprinkler.

Figure 31 represents an elastic plant sprinkler, which every lover of plants should have to syringe or dampen the foliage. They can be had of any seedsman or florist, the cost being $1.25, postpaid.

For heating a bay window, use a coal oil stove, from which there is no smoke or gas. The style of such a stove will be seen represented in figure 32. Place a pan of water on the top to create a moisture, which will be beneficial to the plants.

The price of such a stove is from six to eight dollars, and can be had from any seedsman.

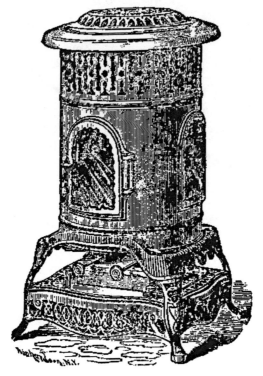

Fig. 32.
Coal Oil Stove.

CHAPTER XX.

For the Azalea use equal parts of loam and peat soil, well mixed and broken with the spade, but not sieved.

I prefer a good, light, fibrous loam, which can be obtained from the hills and fence corners. My sod is cut during the spring and summer, placed in a heap, with grass side down, and in a few weeks it is ready for use.

Peat is a black, sandy soil, and consists of decayed leaves, roots, and sand. I prefer that which is full of fibrous roots. This is cut in sods like that of the loam, but will take a much longer time to decay.

I get this soil in close proximity to my place, and where the wild Azalea abounds. It is better known by the name of swamp honeysuckle.

Had I to procure my peat soil, like many do that send from two to five hundred miles, and some from the Pacific slope, I would, undoubtedly, do without this particular kind of soil.

I am not an advocate for different soils, and so many mixtures, as many recommend.

Use a light and fibrous loam ; always guard against a heavy, clayey soil.

For all plants that I grow, the soil comes from one heap, with the exception of the Daphne, Palm, Erica, and Azalea, and had I not the peat so convenient, they would be grown in the same soil with a little sand added.

4*

Especially for the Azalea, if you have not peat soil, use leaf mould with some sand added. Where leaf mould is not to be had, use one-third sand with loam.

Soil is often blamed for not growing good plants, when the fault is with the grower for not ventilating and syringing properly.

Why do so many Azaleas perish in the hands of amateurs, and why are they so unsuccessful with the cuttings of this plant? Nine-tenths of the Azalea cuttings and plants die from neglect to syringe properly. Red spider is the whole cause of the failure. Sand and soil are seldom in fault.

With me the Azalea and Camellia cuttings are the easiest to grow of my stock, requiring less attention than many of the soft-wooded class of plants.

My advice to the inexperienced is, pay less attention to the mixtures of soil, and more to airing and syringing, and your success will be much better.

CHAPTER XXI.

If you wish to be a successful cultivator of this plant, never use stimulants of any kind, such as liquid manures, fertilizers, &c. I find them in no way beneficial. Give plenty of clean water to the roots when dry, and with frequent syringing over head, they can be grown to perfection.

Give this plant, or the Camellia, liquid manure water, and it will cause them to make rapid growth. They will grow when they should be forming buds. Plants which are grown in this way will not have strength enough to hold up their own foliage without the aid of stakes.

Both the Azalea and Camellia should be grown so as not to require any artificial support.

Lime water is beneficial for this, as well as all other plants which are only re-potted once a year, and many only once in three and five years.

The soil often becomes sour from worms, caused by over-watering or imperfect drainage

Plants will not thrive in such soil. Their roots will soon decay, and the tops will soon follow, and they will have a yellow and sickly appearance.

To keep the ground sweet and free from worms, water three times a year with lime water. Give the plant sufficient to wet every root and fiber, and the hard-wooded plants will be in a good condition. Syringe the foliage four

83

times a year with this water, and it will rid it of many insects.

Receipt for lime water:—Take a flour barrel full of water, add to this one peck of lime. It will be ready for use in ten hours, or as soon as the water becomes cool and clear.

CHAPTER XXII.

There are many opinions as regards sand for rooting cuttings. Some prefer white to black, others river or washed sand, and many must have charcoal dust. All failures to root the cutting are attributed to the color of the sand.

Twenty years ago the washed sand was used by many. Why it was used I am at a loss to say, unless it was washed to clear it of some poisonous mineral or quality which prevented the cuttings from rooting.

I have, at times, a bench of well-rooted cuttings, and occasionally have one that is not so good. I never think of attributing the success or failure to the sand. Have often heard the remark made by visitors, there can be no trouble rooting cuttings in such beautiful white sand.

Some years ago, when looking through florist establishments further north, I saw benches of well-rooted cuttings in sand much darker than that which is found here. I, like many others, gave the sand the credit for the success.

Long since that time, I have given up all such ideas, believing that cuttings can be grown as well in one colored sand as another.

There is no virtue in the color of the sand. It is merely cooling to the wound of the cutting, and will cause it to heal and a callous will form earlier than if placed in soil.

As soon as the cutting is rooted it should be removed

from the sand, as there is nothing in the sand to strengthen or stimulate the young plant.

The failure to root the cutting is more often the fault of the propagator. A branch cut from a plant cannot be placed in the sand bed and form roots without receiving some attention.

The sand should be clean and firmly pressed.

The cuttings require water, shading, airing, and syringing, and for the first few days or until they show signs of recovering, they will need extra attention.

Never attribute the failure to root cuttings to the color of the sand.

Cleanliness of the cutting bed will add greatly to the health of the cuttings,.

Sand which has been used constantly for six or twelve months will become dirty from decayed leaves, &c., and will cause a fungus to grow over the sand bed, which will destroy the cuttings if it is not renewed.

CHAPTER XXIII.

For large plants of Azaleas and Camellias, and others of the hard wood kind that require large pots or tubs, and are not changed or re-potted every season, drainage is very necessary. Without it the ground would become sour by the outlet clogging up, preventing the water, which the plants do not need, from passing off, and causing the roots of large plants to decay.

I never use drainage for soft-wooded plants, or for small pots of the hard wood kind, considering it a waste of time. Use drainage for all hard-wooded plants in pots over eight inches.

Drainage is thought by some a work which can be carelessly done, and have the desired effect. I differ very much in this particular, thinking it a very important matter, and one that should be done with some care, in the following manner. Use a large piece of broken pot or shell over the hole in the bottom of the pot, with smaller pieces over this, finishing up with still smaller pieces of shells or pots, with a covering of moss to prevent the soil from mixing with the drainage.

In looking over my stock I find more plants that require fresh drainage than larger pots.

Imperfect drainage of those plants in large pots or tubs that have been thoroughly saturated with water, will easily be detected by the water remaining on the surface of the

87

ground, and not passing to the roots, or running off as it should.

All such plants should be removed at once from the pot and allowed to dry for ten hours, when they can be replaced in the pot with fresh drainage.

Should such plants be allowed to remain any length of time in imperfect drainage, they will lose their roots, and in a short time die.

CHAPTER XXIV.

There is no reason why red spider should be allowed to destroy the fresh greenness of the leaves of the Azalea, if the directions have been followed for syringing the foliage.

Insects are the cause of disease, therefore watch the plants closely to keep them in a healthy condition, and there will be no fear of a serious attack of any insect.

I find it impossible, with all my care, to keep the Azalea perfectly clear of red spider during the months of March and April, or just before they are removed from the greenhouse to the open air, during the named months. I do not allow this pest to become so numerous that either the plants or foliage are affected by it.

To prevent an increase of red spider, syringe thoroughly to create a moist atmosphere.

Soon after being removed to the open air, red spider will disappear. Keep up the usual amount of syringing with clean water during the summer months, or until the dews are heavy.

Red spider cannot exist in a moist atmosphere, but will increase very rapidly in a hot, dry, or in an untidy house.

Mealy bug will seldom be found on the Azalea, unless syringing has been neglected.

On the old branches of plants ten years and older, will be found a white scale, which in looks resembles the

mealy bug, although it is of an entirely different character.
It can easily be detected by the color, which is a purplish
white. It leaves no white track behind it
like the mealy bug. This insect is very
dangerous when it gets among the
Azaleas.

To destroy this insect use coal oil, and
for distributing the oil, use the floral
atomizer, which is represented in figure 33.

Fig. 33.
Floral Atomizer.

This will eject such a fine spray that the plants will not
be injured in any way by the small quantity of oil they
receive. It will rid the plants of this insect. After this
treatment the Azalea will soon present a healthy appearance.

Coal oil used in any other way than has been directed,
will in all probability prove fatal to the plants.

If clean water is used as often and as thoroughly as has
been recommended, the plants will be perfectly healthy and
never infested with insects to such an extent as to require
syringing with preparations of any kind.

To prevent insects from spreading through the houses,
use the following wash :—One peck of lime, a half pound
of flour of sulphur, stir well together, apply to the pipes
and flues as you would whitewash. It is not necessary to
wash the pipes all around the house. Wash around the
furnace, the middle and extreme ends. It is only the fumes
of the sulphur that is wanted.

This wash will not injure the most delicate plant if used
as directed. Never use dry sulphur on the pipes or flues, as
recommended by some. It will prove fatal to the whole
stock.

CHAPTER XXV.

Any glass structure will be suitable to grow this plant, although some particular styles are better adapted than others.

When building, we all have some object in view, and are guided in the kind of a structure by what we want to grow in it.

For Azaleas, Camellias, and all hard-wooded and specimen plants which are not of rapid growth, I prefer a span roof house, as represented in figure 34. The plants that

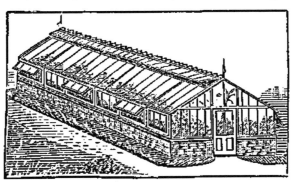

Fig. 34.
House suitable for Azaleas.

I have named only grow from six weeks to two months in the spring. By being grown in this kind of a house they are well shaped. In a lean-to house, hard-wooded plants usually grow one-sided, unless they are turned very often.

Azaleas and Camellias flourish well together. The same

91

temperature will do for both. They also require a moist
atmosphere. Azaleas which are grown in the same temperature as Camellias, will not come into bloom before the
months of February and March.

The house shown in the engraving will answer for
other plants besides those mentioned, always using the
coolest part of the house for Azaleas and Camellias.

Syringe frequently. Moisture will improve the appearance and health of the plants.

For heating such a house, use a boiler and hot water
pipes. The first outlay is but a trifle more than that of the
brick flue system. The plants will be in a much better
condition, and more easily kept in health.

CHAPTER XXVI.

The Azaleas Indica Alba and Amœna have both proved
to be perfectly hardy. They will stand in open borders
without any protection, during our most severe winters,
and will also stand the hot scorching sun of our summers.
These are very unlike the hardy Rhododendron and Azalea
Mollis, both of which require shade, and are generally
found in this climate planted among the shade of trees.

Indica Alba is grown to a great extent in the parks and
cemeteries around New York, and retains its foliage during
winter, blooming through the months of May and June, a
perfect sheet of white flowers. It is a valuable acquisition
to the list of hardy white flowering shrubs.

Azalea Amœna has also proved hardy, and is grown in
open borders in parks, both in the north and south. Like
Indica Alba it retains its foliage during the winter months.

The flowers are small, double, rosy purple, and bloom in
early spring. These will be found admirably adapted for
making clumps on lawns, or for borders, &c.

Where beds are planted exclusively of these two
kinds, Alba should be placed in the centre, and Amœna
on the outer edges, as it is of a more dwarf habit. By so
massing them there will be in the same bed both white and
rosy purple.

For the culture of the Azalea in the open air, use any good garden soil with a light mixture of sand.

Have the beds rather elevated or mounded up, so that the water will not lodge about the roots during the winter months.

As soon as the bloom is over in the spring, trim the plants, cutting back all long branches.

Keep the plants shapely by using the knife freely.

Cut out all small twiggy wood : they are only robbing the strong shoots of the nourishment they require.

The small wood in the centre of the plant produces no flowers, therefore it is of no benefit.

Treated in the way mentioned they will be an ornament to any grounds, and I think preferable to either the Rhododendrons or Mollis Azalea. Neither of these will stand the summer sun, but will grow best in a thicket.

Hardy plants which I consider valuable are those which thrive on an open lawn, where their beauty can be seen when in flower.

CHAPTER XXVII.

Thirty named Azaleas—twenty single and ten double kinds:

These I consider distinct, being chosen from two hundred kinds.

Indica Alba—Single, white.

Baron de Vriere—Salmon rose, dark spots, fine flower.

Beauty of Europe—Pink, striped with carmine.

Bijou de Paris—White, striped rose.

Charles Van Eckhaute—Bright orange, spotted, crimped edges.

Crimeria—Rich crimson.

Coloris Nova—Dark carmine with rich dark spots.

Eulalie Van Ghert—Light rose, spotted with carmine.

Frostii—Violet pink.

Fielder's White—Fine large flower.

Glory of Belgium—White, striped with pink, fringed edges. ·

Hortense Vervaene—Pale flesh color, bordered salmon, vermillion spots.

Iveryana—White, striped and spotted.

John Gould Veitch—Lilac rose.

Madame Ambroise Verschaffeltii.

Marquis of Lorne—Beautiful orange.

Pride of Dorking—Vivid crimson.

Punctulate—Creamy white, spotted and striped cherry red.

Theodore Prusser—Deep rose, shaded violet.

Vesuvius—Large pale orange with dark spots.

TEN BEST DOUBLE AZALEAS, DISTINCT KINDS.

Bernhard Andre—Violet crimson.

Bouquet de Roses—Bright clear rose.

Borsig or Flag of Truce—Both good double whites.

Francois de Vos—Deep crimson scarlet.

Glory of Sunninghill—Salmon.

Jean Vervane—Semi-double, crimson, white and rose.

Madame Iris Lefebvre—Dark orange.

Mlle. Marie Van Houtte—White and salmon.

Rachael Von Varnhagan—Rosy purple.

Souvenir de Prince Albert—White and rose, deeply spotted, superb.

CHAPTER XXVIII.

During the past year some growers have been trying to grow the Azalea after it is one year old from a cutting, by planting them out in beds during the summer months, in the same manner as we would roses or bedding plants. The result of this new practice has been very satisfactory.

They have grown twice the size of those planted in pots, and have produced buds which will, in all probability, flower finely the next season.

Azalea Indica Alba and Amœna have proved to be hardy.

I do not know of any reason why other varieties would not thrive equally as well if planted outside during the summer, although I have never tried it myself. If they would thrive, it would be a profitable way of growing them.

During the next season I expect to plant one or two thousand in open borders as a test, and will give the result of this practice in one of our floral journals. If it proves a success it will be a great saving of labor over the old pot system of growing this plant.

For those wishing to try this experiment, I would advise them to begin on a small scale. Should water be convenient syringe at night for the first three or four weeks; at the end of this time the dews will be sufficient, and the plants will have adhered to the new soil.

Plant in light, sandy soil.

5   97

CHAPTER XXIX.

PACKING AZALEA PLANTS FOR SHIPMENT.—TREATMENT BEST
FOR THEM AFTER THEY ARE RECEIVED.

The wood of these plants is very brittle, therefore some care must be exercised in packing them.

From the first of June until the latter part of September, pack in open boxes as you would any other plants, and with or without the pots. Although those packed without pots will carry in a much better condition, providing the roots are in sufficient number to keep the ball of earth together. The freight or express charges will be much less, which is quite an item.

After the plants are removed from the pots, use dry moss around the ball of earth, then wrap only the ball in brown paper. It is not necessary to have the whole plant covered with paper.

When plants of either the Camellia or Azalea are received without pots during the fall, or whenever the buds are formed, place them back in the same or nearly the same size pots as they were in before being shipped. A larger size pot and fresh soil at this time will cause many of them to cast their buds and begin to grow. The result will be no flowers the coming season.

If received in the spring when the plants are growing, or about to show their young growth, and the ball is well matted with roots, a size larger pot will be necessary, and it will, in fact, greatly benefit the plants.

Should the plants arrive in a very dry condition, which is often the case (after being packed for twenty or thirty days), soak both the ball of roots and the tops in water for ten hours, after which place in pots, giving them a shady place for a few days.

It will be much better to receive plants that have suffered from drought, than those which have had too much moisture, for they will become damp and mouldy. When in this condition there is no treatment known that will restore them to their former health.

Do not disturb or unpack plants which are received in cold weather in a frozen state. Keep them in a dark place where the thermometer ranges about forty-five degrees, until all signs of frost have left them, when they can be unpacked and potted. Syringe the foliage and keep them in a partially shaded place for a few days longer, then they should be watered at the roots.

CHAPTER XXX.

January.

During this month your plants will need careful watching, as regards airing, watering, and syringing. Generally the weather is very cold, and a greater amount of artificial heat is necessary to keep the frost out of the house. When the day is fine, admit a little air between the hours of 11 a.m. and 2 p.m.

Open the sash or ventilator according to the temperature you have in the house, although the weather may be cold and freezing. If the sun is bright, your house may mark one hundred; such is too high a temperature. A little air can be given without having your plants *chilled*. Do not pull your sash half way down; one or two inches will be of great benefit to the plants.

Never omit airing your house in fine weather. Azaleas which are *blooming*, and kept at a high temperature, will require syringing twice a day, night and morning. Those that are in the cooler houses will require syringing once a day, and let it be done during the morning.

Water all plants that require it, and let it be done during the early part of the day, that the plants may *absorb* it and become partially dry before night.

Keep all dead foliage from the plants. Water during this month once with *lime water*. Give them enough to wet

100

every root and fiber, and let no plant *escape*, wet or dry. This is done to kill the worms and keep the ground sweet.

February.

The days will be getting longer, and the sun more powerful.

Air your plants freely when the day will admit. Many will be flowering and making young wood towards the last of the month.

Young stocks which were rooted last May should now be in fine condition to graft, and should be grafted while the wood is young. The named *kinds* which were rooted last May will now require one size larger pot, and the tops nipped from the young shoots, to cause them to *bush*.

Your grafted plants which were worked last February and March, will have a great tendency again to throw out shoots below the graft. Cut all such off. Syringe as for last month.

March.

Air freely and syringe often. Towards the end of this month your glass will need a slight shade on it to keep the sun from burning the foliage. Most of your plants will be in full bloom, and making young wood. Give them sufficient water when dry to wet them thoroughly, but only water those that require it. Do the balance of your grafting this month, and begin re-potting those plants that flowered last month.

Prepare your sand boxes for the cuttings, and have everything in readiness. Keep as little artificial heat this

month as practicable. Trim all plants this month. Cut
back the long branches, and cut out the twiggy wood. Get
your plants shapely. Water your plants at this time in
the afternoon or evening.

April.

Your plants, if in health, should be growing finely, and
the balance of your stock in flower. Give plenty of air
during this month, also room on the benches, that they may
form well. Re-pot balance of your stock which was not
attended to last month. Take cuttings this month. Those
plants which were grafted in February will all be firmly
united, and the cord which held the graft in place should be
removed, and the glass removed from the frame. Give
them one size larger pots. Rub all shoots off which appear
below the graft. Allow nothing to grow but the newly-
inserted graft. Syringe twice a day. Red spider and
thrip will make their appearance, notwithstanding all the
syringing and dampening of the house. Your plants will
need more water as the season advances. Look over them
daily.

May.

Get your plants to the open air as early as possible this
month, or red spider and thrip will make sad work. Place
them outside, as directed before, on a wet day, and plunge
the pots to the rim. A shady place will not be required.

Your young grafted plants can also be put out in the
open air.

Towards the end of this month the cuttings which were
placed in the sand first part of April will be rooted, and

require soil and pots. Remove these to frames as directed elsewhere. Syringe all Azaleas twice a day, that are outside, until the night dews are heavy, when syringing can be dispensed with.

June, July and August.

All your plants should at this time be in the open air, and the pots plunged. When the weather is warm, and no dews at night, syringe twice a day. Watch the young grafted plants, for they will still have a great tendency to throw out young shoots below the graft. Nothing further is required during these three months. Syringe, water when dry, and keep your plants free from dead leaves, branches, &c., &c.

September.

Towards the end of this month, and before the first frost, have all your plants brought to the house. Give them a light top dressing of fresh soil. See that they are clear of all insects. Give all the plants a dose of lime water after removing them to the house. Place your young cuttings on benches, and as near the glass as possible. Syringe once or twice a day. Those plants that you wish for early flowering remove to the forcing house.

October.

Your plants should be all housed. Give them water at the roots only when dry. Those that are in the forcing house syringe twice a day. Give plenty of air in fine weather, it will add much to the health and vigor of your plants.

The seeds which were ripe and gathered last month should now be sown in pans or boxes, as has been directed.

November and December.

Air when the weather will permit.   Fresh air will do more for your plants during these months than any stimulant you can give them.   Syringe as for October.   Keep pinching the tops off the young plants which were rooted last spring.   Look over your young grafts, and keep the suckers down.   Syringe with lime water.

CHAPTER XXXI.

I have named in a previous chapter twenty (20) distinct single Azaleas, also ten (10) double. I will now give a full list, as is published in many catalogues. About one third of them I consider distinct and worth growing, the balance are good, but too much alike when in flower to be classed as distinct kinds.

Alba, white, the best for early flowering.

Admiration, white, striped.

Adelina, red, semi-double.

Alba, Illustrious Plena, white, double.

Alba Multiflora, white, blotched and striped.

Alba Plena, white, double.

Alba Striata, white, striped.

Alexander, white, striped, edges fringed.

Alice, rose, blotched, vermillion, double.

Amœna, rosy purple, double, hardy.

Amœna Grandiflora, rosy purple, large flowered.

Amœna IIybrida, rosy pink.

Andersonii, rich rosy carmine.

Apollo, deep scarlet.

Ardens, bright orange scarlet.

Armide, white.

Arelia, white and purple.

Arborea Purpurea, large, purple, double.

Athenerman, bright rosy pink.

Auguste Van Geert, semi-double, color satiny rose.

Auguste Delfosse, dark orange, shaded buff.

Baron de Pret, rosy lilac.

Baron de Vriere, salmon rose, large flowered.

Baron Ed Osy, bright orange.

Baron Hruby, lilac, tinted with white.

Beauty of Reigate, white, spotted rose.

Beauty of Europe, pink, striped carmine.

Bernhard Andre, Alba, white double.

Belle Grantoise, rosy salmon.

Bijou de Paris, white, striped carmine.

Bouquet de Roses, clear rose, double.

Borsig, white. double, one of the best.

Bride, large, waxy white.

Brookleyana, white, striped.

Carl Petzold, dark carmine.

Charmer, bright carmine.

Charles Enke, rose, edged with white.

Charles Van Eckhaute, orange spotted, crimped edges.

Columbia, white, striped violet.

Coloris Nova, dark carmine.

Comet, salmon scarlet.

Countess de Flanders, bright rose, large flowered.

Criterion, rose, edged white.

Crimeria, rich crimson.

Dame Melanie, bright rose, edge white.

Dante, bright red.

Danielsiana, orange red.

Dieudonne Spae, clear rose.

Dr. Augustin, large, deep red.

Dr. Lindley, orange, maroon blotches.

Dr. Livingstone, deep rose.

Duke of Wellington, bright scarlet.

Duc de Malakoff, bright rose, double.

Duc de Nassau, rich crimson.

Eclipse, bright crimson.

Egregia, plum color.

Emperor, orange scarlet.

Etna, brilliant crimson.

Eloile de Gand, salmon, white margin.

Eugenie Mazel, rosy lilac.

Eulalie Van Ghert, pink and blush, spotted.

Eulalie Van Ghert, Variegata, foliage variegated, flowers pink and blush.

Extraneii, violet rose.

Fascination, rosy pink, edged white.

Fielder's White, white, large flower.

Flag of Truce, white, large and double.

Formosa, deep red.

Francois de Vos, scarlet double.

Frederick Schleiermacher, bright pink, with metalic tint.

Frederick der Grosse, dark rose, shaded purple.

Frostii, violet pink.

Franklin, white, striped crimson.

Frau Cassian, white, spotted and striped.

Gledstanesia, white, striped.

Glory of Arras, bright rose, white margin.

Glory of Belgium, white, striped and spotted.

Glory of Sunninghill, salmon double.

Grossfurstin Helene, salmon, with rich dark spots.

Grata, rich vermillion.

Hermann Seidel, bright rose, double.

Hermine, white, carmine stripes, double.

Hercules, dark red.

Her Majesty, rosy lilac, edged white.

Henrich Liesmeyer, brilliant orange, scarlet.

Hortense Vervaene, pale flesh, marked with white and salmon.

Illustrious, orange scarlet.

Imbricata, white, spotted rose, double.

Imperial, red.

Imperatrice Josephine, purplish rose.

Indica Alba, single, white.

Iveryana, white, striped rose.

Jean Van Geert, bright glossy rose.

Jean Verschaffelt, deep orange, shaded.

Konigen Louis Von Preussen, rosy red.

Lateritia, salmon, habit very dwarf.

Lateritia Alba, white

La Victoria, deep orange, blotched.

Leava, white.

Leuco Majestica, white.

Lovely, white, striped purple.

Louis Napoleon, rosy purple.

Louis Margottin, greenish white, striped with crimson.

Madam Amber Verschaffelt, white, striped.

Madam Alex. Langenhone, variegated, white, speckled rose.

Madam Camilie Van Langenhone, snow white, striped crimson.

Madam Dom Vervaene, rose, striped lilac.

Madam Michael, white, striped purple.

Madam Miellez, large, white, lilac stripe.

Madam Gus Lefebvre, dark orange, double.

Madam Verschaffelt, violet, rose-shaded white.

Marquis of Lorne, beautiful orange.

Magniflora, salmon, white margin.

Maitlandii, white, striped and spotted.

Magnet, rosy salmon.

Minerva, rich orange scarlet.

Mlle. Maria Van Houtte, striped, double.

Mr. Fry, bright carmine.

Narcissiflora, white, double.

Napoleon III, deep orange.

Ne Plus Ultra, orange scarlet.

Neptune, orange, shaded violet.

Nonpariel, white, ribboned rose.

Optima, orange scarlet.

Ovata, light lilac.

Pauline Mardeur, bright rose, double.

Perfection, bright rose, spotted.

Phœnicia, large, purple.

President Clayes, dark salmon, margined white.

President Victor Van den Hecke, white, mottled and striped
 rose.

Prince Alex. Von Hessen, salmon, shaded white.

Princesse Alexandre, white, striped crimson.

Princesse Charlotte, deep rose, red blotched.

Professor Koch, deep pink, double.

Pride of Dorking, vivid crimson.

Punctulata, creamy white, spotted and striped.

Queen Victoria, white, purple striped.

Rachael Von Varnhagan, rosy purple.

Reine des Beauties, salmon rose, semi-double.

Reine des Pays Bas, striped, crimson.

Reine des Belges, rosy pink.

Roi Leopold, rich salmon.

Roi des Beauties, fine rose, white margin.

Rubra Plena, red, double.

Rubens, bright orange scarlet.

Semi-duplex Maculata, rose, semi-double.

Sigismund Rucker, lilac rose, margined white.

Souvenir de l'Exposition, delicate pink, white margin.

Souvenir de Prince Albert, white and rose, semi-double.

Stanleyana, rose-shaded carmine.

Stella, pale orange.

Superba, bright red.

Tannhauser, deep red.

Theresia, orange, blotched.

Theodore Prussen, deep rose, shaded violet.

Toilete de Flore, white, striped.

Triomphe de Mainz, rosy scarlet.

Triomphe de Gand, clear salmon.

Variegata, rose, margined white, dwarf habit.

Vesta, white.

Vesuvius, large, pale orange.

Vittata Punctuatta, white, striped.

Vittata Fortunii, white, striped purple.

Vittata Rosea, rose colored.

Van Hartwig, light red.

William Bull, large, rose, semi-double.

Wilhelm Tell, carmine, striped.

Camellia Culture

CONTENTS OF CAMELLIA CULTURE.

COLORED PLATES.

CAMELLIA JAPONICA.—

Single Red.
Alba Plena.—Double White.
Imbricata.—Crimson and White.
Sarah Frost.—Rosy Crimson.

BOOKS ON FLORICULTURE.

I have frequent inquiries as to which are the best books for beginners, and those who are seeking general information as regards Floriculture, &c.

I have read the following works, and have found they contain more practical knowledge and information than any other books that have yet been issued from the American press.

GARDENING FOR PROFIT.

A guide to the successful cultivation of the market and family garden.

BY PETER HENDERSON.

GARDENING FOR PLEASURE.

A guide to the amateur in the fruit, vegetable, and flower garden, with full directions for the greenhouse, conservatory, and window garden.

BY PETER HENDERSON.

PRACTICAL FLORICULTURE.

A guide to the successful cultivation of the florist's plants. For the amateur and professional florist.

BY PETER HENDERSON.

Price of each book, post-paid, $1.50, and can be had of any seedsman.

CPSIA information can be obtained at www.ICGtesting.com
Printed in the USA
LVOW130840171212

311952LV00001BA/8/P